Public Speaking Greatness

Power Communication to Your Advantage

By

David K. Ewen, M.Ed.

ISBN: 9798406299333

Imprint: Enterprise College

www.EnterpriseCollege.org

Cover theme background
El Cap, Yosemite National Park, United States
Produced by: Adam Cool
Published on March 17, 2015

www.EnterpriseCollege.org

David K. Ewen, M.Ed.

<u>Ambassador Professor</u>

Enterprise College

www.EnterpriseCollege.org

Contents

About the Book

Public Speaking Greatness brings the tips, tricks, and techniques to improve your public speaking style to greater performance to bring greater impact to your audiences. The methods brought on by an international award-winning educator will change your stance in the public arena.

<u>About the author</u>

The acclaimed sought-after international award-winning David K. Ewen, M.Ed., an acclaimed educator since 1988, an entrepreneur since 1994, an Ambassador Professor since 2015 and ordained minister since 2021, has been a professional speaker in front of LIVE audiences, classrooms, broadcast radio, streaming podcast, and at church altars.

David is the author of several books and audiobooks on a variety of professional issues. David's specialty is in global communications and entrepreneurial studies. In addition to speaking in front of live audiences, he creates and presents classroom workshop seminars and online masterclass webinars.   In the EdTech industry (education technology), David is a content creator developing curriculum which he presents in online coaching sessions and masterclass webinars.   He earned a master's degree in Education with a concentration in management and attended post graduate studies in business administration before he launched his publishing company in

July 1994.

David K. Ewen, M.Ed.

Ambassador Professor

Enterprise College

www.EnterpriseCollege.org

<u>Introduction</u>

One of the most important professional skills, if not the most important, is public speaking. Communication is key to any entrepreneurial and business success. Public speaking comes in a variety of forms and knowing how to do it right is key for success.

It is true that you don't get a second chance to make a first impression.

Take advantage of diving into the tips, tricks, and techniques to become successful in public speaking. It is worth the effort to develop the skill so that you can benefit from the advantage. Your competitive edge is your communication skills. Make the best out of it.

Early Experience

From an early child up through the first four years of running my business, I was dreadfully afraid of speaking in front of an audience. What broke the ice was the absolute need to be public as part of my business at the time. As the founding director of the New England Publishers Association (NEPA), I happened to be immersed in radio broadcasting on a morning show simulcasted on WORC 1310 AM and WGFP 940 AM.   Properly located in central New England of the United States, this weekly broadcast on Thursdays interviewing authors put my voice to the public for the first time.   I learned how to put presentations together.

The radio show was followed by a one-year tour of various publishing industry conferences as a speaker representing NEPA while promoting the self-publishing and independent press industry. I learned about audience styles in different geographic areas.

Later in 2004, I thought it good to teach book publishing at colleges as it had already been 10 years since I had launched my publishing company. It was Saturday, June 12, 2004, at 9:00 in the morning at Holyoke Community College in Massachusetts, USA when I attended my first assignment as visiting professor. A controversial student managed to split the class with some defending my authority in publishing and the other half rebuking it. I survived the workshop seminar with lessons for the future about controlling and audience. This type of catastrophe never happened again.

My early experience taught me (1) how to put presentations together (2) different geographic areas have demographics and economics that make audience members different (3) and how to control an audience. What I learned in my early years of public speaking are rudimentary, but served as founding principles to grow on.   This foundation created me as a professional public speaker today as well as a successfully published author.

<u>Examples to Follow</u>

Many public speakers learn from others. For me, it was Steve Jobs, the founder of Apple.   The way he showed command of the audience by pacing the stage to show his territory.   That was emphasized by the hand and arm gestures.

When I took lessons from what I learned from Jobs, I noticed that pacing the stage caused audience heads to turn and that motion kept the audience interested.   There is something about a change of scenery that a speaker can present by not standing in one place.   I also learned that a sense of humor to get the audience to chuckle or laugh goes a long way.   The laughing opens the lungs to more oxygen helping keep the audience alert and more awake. This keeps

the audience more attentive.

Online Presence

Before talking about public speaking methodology, let's first talk about the online presence of digital footprint of a professional public speaker. I don't lean toward Facebook, but perhaps a Facebook page is OK. I'm more interested in a professional social sharing site like LinkedIn where the profile is very much like a CV or resume with posting of professional activity. On the other hand, Facebook fits a more general mainstream community. If your genre fits that, then, Facebook would be good. I would suggest Twitter to take advantage of its microblogging format with searchable features of hashtags. Postings on Twitter can be set in advance through ***Tweet Deck*** and simple ads can be placed for broader presence. Ads can be placed on LinkedIn too.   Aside from that, a personal website using tools such as sites.Google.com and getting a domain name from google ensures a solidly hosted site that is easy to make.   There are many other competitive tools for do-it-yourself website development.

<u>Overcoming Nervous Behavior</u>

Well of course, the topic of being nervous is common when talking about public speaking. Addressing it is often easier said than done.   It seems the people who aren't nervous think they have all the answers about overcoming nervousness in public speaking. The fact is all people are different in the way they handle it.   Some people are natural public speakers while others must overcome the fear. No two people are the same.

I address the issue in terms of a mindset. Jumping into cold water can be scary. But once you hit the water, the immediate shock passes so fast that you are no longer thinking of the cold. The adrenaline in your body helps you adjust to the temperature change.

The same can be said about Olympic athletes.   There is the normal professional athletic industry anxiety that is overcome by being in the moment and blocking out everything else.   That focused attention brought on by adrenaline is what makes the athlete succeed. The initial onset of adrenaline before the competition is what puts the nervous feeling of butterflies in your stomach.   Well, this happens with public speakers.

The nervous adrenaline of public speakers puts that natural feeling of nervous butterflies in your stomach. That may edge up the nervous anxiety.   Those effects can be put in control by being aware that these feelings are normal and expected. Control the anxiety by a slow controlled breathing. Help your dry mouth by drinking room temperature water. Cold or hot water will change your voice and you don't want to do that. Make sure you moisten your nervous dry mouth with room temperature water. Carry a bottle with you.

Later, we will talk about preparing for rehearsals. It's those rehearsals that help reduce if not eliminate severe anxiety. The reason is rehearsals make sure that the real presentation isn't actually the first time. This puts you in a place of familiarity and comfort knowing that you've done the presentation before.

<u>Handouts For Audience</u>

There is always a one-page handout that I give audience members.   Information at the top serves as my business card. I don't have to worry about running out of business cards or having enough on hand. It's easy to make basic copies of a one pager of content that reveals what is to be presented.   In addition to the agenda, special information such as key websites, acronyms, or other references should all fit nicely on one page. Very often, audience members will write notes on the back giving that one pager more value.

Obvious Eye Contact

Its obvious eye contact is a strong element of public speaking. Direct eye contact with audience members keeps them alert as if speaking directly to that person. The same effect happens to audience members around that person. The emotion seen in the eyes can demonstrate trust of what is being presented. Hidden eyes or eyes that dash away from the audience show a sense of fear and generate a lack of trust from the audience members.

Speakers who still have hesitancy to make eye contact can trace their eyes just above the head of the audience toward the back wall.   A momentary glance to one side and switching to the other side of the room will give the effect of making eye contact with the room. This is aided by not being stationary and pacing the stage to show authority.

Body Language & Gestures

The audience is not just looking at your eyes. They are also looking at how you stand and use hand gestures. Your posture says a lot about your confidence. A stand-up straight kind of guy looks so much better than being hunched over. The hands and arms must be open and expressive to the words being said. They should not be folded or held together putting up a fence between you and the audience. The audience picks up on that and can see nervous body language. It takes time to practice a style that fits best for you that involves not standing in one place and using hands to emphasize points. Online videos of Corporate CEOs or professional sport coaches and more can help you shop around for ideas that fit your style of body language and hand gestures. Think about movements that prevent you from standing in one place. A pacing of the stage to some extent shows authority as the speaker should own the stage. I used Steve Jobs style to teach me about hand gestures and walking with confidence.

Using Written Notes

Of course, some sort of a set of notes is needed to ensure smoothness of content. The elementary school style of face down on paper reading word for word sounds robotic and disconnected from the audience. Quite simply, it doesn't work. It shows a sense of being unprepared and reduces the speaker to one who does not know what he or she is talking about. It's quite embarrassing.

In my early days of public speaking, I used index cards with a basic outline or list of topics to ensure I didn't miss any element to be presented. The content presentation was reliant on what I already knew and didn't have to read. Years later, as a college professor, I put a list of up to 20 topics on the far-right side of the white board and used that as my guide.

There are times when nearly word-for-word text is needed to follow. It's just like a teleprompter used for a presidential speech.   The same effect can be created without a teleprompter.   The content can be printed in large text with a space between sentences.   The pages are put in sheet protectors and placed in a binder.   As the pages are turned, the sheet protectors provide good finger grip.   The ringed binder makes for easy page turning.   Within the text, after each sentence, there is a line to break each sentence separately.   This helps prevent getting lost in crowded text.

With the evolution of technology, the ringed binder with clear sheet protectors have been replaced with a tablet computer or laptop displaying a scrolling PDF file. As before, the text has sentences with a space above and below to ensure not getting lost in crowded text.

Content Organization

The best way to think about how to organize the presentation of spoken content is to think about the chapter of a book.   The table of contents would represent the introduction to show promise of what is to come. Each chapter stands alone in terms of completeness with a clear statement followed by a set of examples or clarifications and ends with a closing understanding.

As one chapter concludes and another is presented, there are transitional spoken phrases such as, "That is all I have to say about X. Now I am going to talk about Y". Anything can be done to ensure acknowledgement that one chapter has ended, and another is to begin.

It is best to include in the conclusion the agenda that was mentioned in the introduction. That agenda for the introduction was the promise to come. As part of the conclusion, it is a demonstration that the promise was kept and that the presentation is whole and complete. Again, think of the agenda as a table of contents with chapters. Each chapter represents the different topics in the

presentation.

<u>Knowing Your Stuff</u>

Sure, we can talk about elements of key contact, using notes, and content, but there is nothing that replaces knowing what you are talking about. If you don't then you are following a script and it will show in your face and body language.   You can't fool the audience.   The notes are a set of train tracks, but your knowledge is the powerful train that must work

when riding those train tracks.

Prepare with Rehearsals

Professional speakers constantly rehearse because you never get a second chance to make a first impression. The presentation has to be done right the first time. It also has to look like it was not the first time. There is a way you can make that happen.

Using Audacity as an audio recording tool and Anchor.FM as a podcast platform distributing to Spotify, you can create a podcast as your first run through. You can search YouTube videos on how to use Audacity and get the free open-sourced download here: www.AudacityTeam.org/download

Spotify owns Anchor.FM so that is why posting on Anchor puts your podcast on Spotify.

To go beyond your first trial run or rehearsal, videos can be recorded on your laptop or computer using the site webcamera.io and a virtual background can be generated using the tool from chromacam.me. The video can be recorded, downloaded, and then uploaded to YouTube as a public or private video.

Usually, two rehearsals via podcast and video is sufficient for the final run-through of a presentation.   It gives you enough to understand what needs to be changed in your text and usually it is something to be   deleted.   Often,   our presentation is too much with too many examples and clarifications. Sometimes it's best to be direct and to the point.   The audience is smarter than we all think.

The rehearsal process gives you a feel for the text and helps you practice a more natural flow as you use the text as a guide. Sometimes improvement to the natural flow of using the text may require increasing the text size so that your eyes don't struggle to find what is written. You may also find that something needs to be changed to go along with a natural way of saying something that is different from the proper way of

writing it.

<u>Speaker Authenticity</u>

A good presenter, professor, mentor, or coach has something called speaker authenticity. What is that? Well, it's having a book and audiobook published. A good speaker shows authenticity by being published. Famous research scientists are highly recognized because they are published in respected and well known scientific journals. We aren't all research scientists, but our authenticity must be presented through published works. Today's publishing industry has books published in hardcover, paperback, eBook, and audiobook. The audiobook is a form of public speaking, and it brings the text to life.

<u>Event Planning</u>

Before a presentation, a Meet and Greet is suggested to get to know the audience.   I usually have 30 minutes set before the presentation to allow me to know a few or more audience members.   This familiarity with a person or two in the audience helps reduce that nervous anxiety because it is those people who add a sense of familiarity with the audience. You also have a sense of what the audience is looking for and dynamically you can adjust closing comments or other parts of the presentation to cater to those needs.

The one-pager hand out containing agenda and key elements help the audience remember what was presented. The backside is often used by the audience to write notes, especially the answer to the questions that they or others might ask.

I reserve the last 15 or 20 minutes for Q & A (Questions and Answers). This way, whatever goal the audience did not achieve in my presentation, then they have that opportunity. This ensures that the presentation satisfies the needs of the audience. After all, that is the goal to satisfy the needs of the audience. Some inexperienced presenters make the mistake of focusing on what they want to say and satisfying their own needs.

It's best to plan the event to include three elements. (1) The meet and greet to get familiar and comfortable with the audience. (2) Handing out a one pager with agenda and key elements to help guide the audience through the presentation. And (3) the Q & A in the last 15 to 20 minutes to ensure the audience gets all the satisfaction they need and that you as a speaker reach audience expectations.

Published Speaker

An authenticated speaker is one who has a published book. The book marks a speaker as a subject matter expert. All top speakers, mentors, coaches, business leaders, and professors have a book published. It goes with the territory that a professional speaker is also a published author. It's the book that originally makes the speaker professional. It's the book that authenticates the speaker.

The next several chapters are an excerpt from The Complete Guide to Self Publishing that only show the publishing of hardcover, paperback, ebook and audiobooks.

Audiobooks are important for a professional speaker as they contain content in the author's voice. Moreover, audiobooks bring text to life with the professional speaker's voice.

Format of Book

The format and construction of books in the modern age come in the following:

- Paperback

- Hardcover

- eBook (digital)

- Audiobook (digital)

Two of the formats, paperback and hardcover, are physical formats that can be designed for both just once and at the same time utilizing the print-on-demand aggregator publishing resource we'll discuss later. That is the previously mentioned Kindle Direct Publishing platform from Amazon. Please make a mental note that the hardcover version of the book will have a different ISBN number from the paperback version of the book. ISBN stands for International

Standard Book Number. The ISBN is a unique identifier for books. It's like any government issued ID person and unique as each person's thumbprint.

There is no need to wonder whether hardcover or paperback is preferred. It's OK to do both. Each one will get its own unique ISBN and barcode because they are constructed differently.

The other two formats are digital. They are eBook formats for ereaders, tablets, and phones and the other are audiobook format accessible on any digital device.

The three formats that can be produced at the same time using Amazon's Kindle Direct Publishing are paperback, hardcover and eBook.

The Audiobook format is created with a specific set of criteria and distributed through three independently owned aggregators. They are ACX, Authors Republic, and Findaway Voices. ACX is an Amazon company. In 2021, Author's Republic was bought out by RB Media. Also in 2021, Spotify bought out Findaway Voices. These acquisitions will help fuel the continued growth and evolution of the audiobook industry.   It's important for authors of books to take advantage of audiobook publishing using the free resources. Audiobooks give print books life by putting voice to them.

<u>Audiobook Format</u>

The audiobook format that is voice recorded with a specific set of criteria in file format.   Similar to Amazon's Kindle Direct Publishing, free to use publishing aggregator platforms for audiobooks are available. The three platforms are:

- ACX.com

- AuthorsRepublic.com

- FindawayVoices.com

ACX is Audio Creation Exchange from Amazon placing titles on Amazon, Audible and iTunes. Those are the premier destinations of quality content given the strict guidelines of ACX.

Authors Republic is now owned by RB Media as of 2021.

Findaway Voices is owned by Spotify pushing Spotify into the audiobook realm in 2021.

Both Authors Republic and Findaway Voices offer a path to what ACX offers, but it is advisable not to do so. It is preferable to go through ACX directly with **non-exclusive** rights to content allowing distribution through Authors Republic and Findaway Voices to reach a huge arena of audiobook online retail outlets. Audiobook distribution should be carried with non-exclusive rights to a broader retail audience by aggregating content through ACX, Authors Republic and Findaway Voices.

More later on the file format and criteria for producing audiobooks. Suffice to say for now, audiobooks are an important part of a publisher's distribution regimen for content. It is no longer just paperback, hardcover, and eBook.

Audiobook production is a way to give print and eBooks life by putting voice to what was written. The audiobook realm fills the space between written books and movies. This middle space is sufficient to help an author give life to the book they have written by putting voice to it.

The audiobook industry is booming with a lot of changes in the year 2021. Findaway (parent of Findaway Voices) was acquired by Spotify. Authors Republic had been independent, but now is owned by RB Media.

With soundbars, smart speakers, Bluetooth earbuds, wearable smart tech, Android Auto (in cars), and Apple CarPlay (in cars) and much more on the way, it is surely expected that audiobooks will continue to grow as the distribution to consumers becomes easier.

With four formats available and free publishing aggregators with a split revenue share model, it is a necessity that publishers today take advantage of the zero-risk option of publishing at the same time with content produced in paperback, hardcover, eBook, and audiobook. It's great to see a book on an Amazon page showing all four formats displayed together.

Many authors have the desire to have their book become the next best movie or TV show.   We all want that, but the reality is not every single book published will have resources to adequately produce a movie.

The beauty of audiobooks is that authors and publishers can almost be there and enjoy the distribution of their content as a performance presentation. Think of audiobooks filling the space between the written word and the movie. That space is growing due to growth in technology such as smart speakers and Bluetooth connectivity to cars, and more.

At zero cost an author can produce their own narration (with of course a specific set of recording and formatting criteria to be explained later).   It is exciting to produce such content that can easily be done at home just in the same way the book was written.

Although formatting and criteria of audiobooks will be discussed later, it is important at this juncture to clearly acknowledge the importance of audiobooks to authors and publishers.

In many ways the audiobook merges publishing houses and

record labels into one type of business combining the skills from both sides.   This is an example of how authors and small publishers are growing up in a world of technology.

Kindle Direct Publishing

Kindle Direct Publishing or KDP is Amazon owned which is the reason why getting print-on-demand or digital content on Amazon is free using a split revenue share model. KDP is used to set up content in paperback, hardcover, and eBook formats. When represented on the Amazon page, the book shows each format and pricing.

The reason KDP is free to use is because it is 100% self-service. Even getting an ISBN and barcode is free. The print-on-demand merchandise has a revenue share split of 30% to the author/publisher and 70% to Amazon. That is very reasonable given the free ISBN and easy access to the Amazon website.

An advantage of the Print on Demand feature of paperback and hardcover book availability is there is not storage cost, and the book never goes out of print.   Changes can be made later after publishing and that's an advantage.

Now there are other print-on-demand aggregator companies, but you have to pay significantly up front.   The author/publisher takes the risk up front rather than offering a split revenue share model.   For this reason, our focus will be on KDP rather than competitors.

KDP has an expanded distribution that slightly reduces the author/publisher share of the revenue, but it is worth it.   The expanded distribution option, that is a selectable option, allows for books produced on KDP to be made available to other retail outlets such as libraries or bookstores.

Expanded distribution in KDP allows for a greater reach to consumers. It's great to be able to say your book is available wherever books are sold, and people can ask for it at any bookstore. The book may not be on the shelf in the bookstore, but to say that consumers can ask for it to be ordered does in a way make the book accessible to any bookstore.

Along with both print and digital formats, it's a great phrase for authors to say that books are available wherever books are sold. That means both online and in stores. The printed copies are available in both online and offline retail outlets especially when using the KDP expanded distribution option.

A nice thing about KDP is the file format of the document to be uploaded is MS Word, which could likely be in the format originally written in. Storage for safety can be with Docs in Google. If Apple is the preference, pages format can be saved as Docx.

Before uploading the manuscript, remember to have the ISBN requested from KDP (it's instantaneous) and add it to the copyright page.

Most independent press books are with a trim size of 6 inches by 9 inches.   That layout can be set up in Word and then chosen in KDP.

Page numbering alternates on pages. Odd page numbers are right justified and even page numbers are left justified. The even page number that is left justified also includes the title of the book in the header. The odd page number that is right justified also includes the author's name.

The three things to make sure you have corrected before uploading are:

- ISBN on copyright page

- Trim Size in Word matches KDP

- Page numbers formatted correctly

The cover can be created externally with a given specification from KDP.

More conveniently, there is a self-service cover creator.   A picture can be uploaded as part of the cover, but there are free-to-use images that can be used as well. Remember to have an author photo to use for the back cover.   You'll also need to include information about both the author and the book to be included in the back cover as well as online description on retail outlets.

When setting the price within the KDP platform, this is where expanded distribution is selected allowing the book to be available to other online and offline retail outlets and libraries.

Always remember to select expanded distribution when setting the price. It gives the opportunity for the book to be everywhere.

It's great to say in a podcast or radio interview that the book is available wherever books are sold, and you can ask for it at any bookstore. That can only be said if expanded distribution is selected within KDP when setting the price. Granted KDP takes a slightly greater percentage, but it's definitely worth it to have a broad distribution available to other channels such as Barnes and

Noble, other bookstores, libraries, and other online retail outlets.

<u>Audiobook Recording</u>

Audiobook recording has a specific set of criteria necessary to be followed to pass the quality checks of distributor aggregator platforms. ACX from Amazon has the strictest requirements and should be followed for all platforms to have the best success of distribution.

ACX is Audio Creation Exchange owned by Amazon with distribution to Amazon as a companion to at least an eBook on Amazon. One requirement of the audiobook is that at least an eBook should be available. After having discussed KDP, then it's obvious that a paperback, hardcover, and eBook format of the book will be available.

Other platforms are Authors Republic now owned by RB Media as of 2021 and Findaway Voices now owned by Spotify as of 2021. Both have wide range distribution inside and beyond traditional outlets, so both should be taken advantage of.

ACX will hold non-exclusive rights for Amazon, Audible, and iTunes distribution. It's important that you select the option related to non-exclusive rights so that distribution can also be done through Authors Republic and Findaway Voices.

The platforms for distribution are:

- https://www.acx.com/

- https://www.authorsrepublic.com/

- https://findawayvoices.com/

The platform for authors to record narration of their books is Audacity. There are others, but here we'll talk about Audacity because it is free, and we can talk about the specific requirements to create audio content that can pass strict quality checks.

Audacity for Audiobook Recording

Audacity is a free open-source software established many years ago with a lot of tutorial videos online.   It's easy to learn about the high-level details by searching.

What we'll do here is give specific criteria and settings that are specific to audiobook creation.   This will eliminate a lot of the trial and error.

Many people use Audacity for recording and mixing music.   It's different for audiobooks because it is spoken word.   Music and spoken word have different audio recording criteria and requirements.   The attention here is all about spoken word as it relates to creating tracks for audiobooks.

Keep in mind extra tracks are created such as:

- Title and author (few seconds)

- Opening credits

- Opening track

- Record chapters separately

- Closing track

- Closing credits

- Sample track

The sample track is kind of a trailer that is added to the listing of the audiobook in the online retail outlet such as Amazon or Audible.

There is a separate plugin called 'ACX Check' that must be added to Audacity to so that you can do your own quality check before submission. Information on finding and installing ACX Check can easily be found on online video searches.   Just search for "ACX Check for Audiobooks" and you'll find a lot of videos.

Let's start with some important websites.

Download Audacity:

https://www.audacityteam.org/download/

Manual Guide:

https://manual.audacityteam.org/

Learn from others:

https://forum.audacityteam.org/

ACX Check Plugin

https://wiki.audacityteam.org/wiki/Nyquist_Analyze_Plug-ins

Conduct online search for "installing Audacity". You will see simple instructions. Do the same for installing the ACX Check Plugin. This plugin is used to verify quality of audiobook recorded content in the three following areas:

- Peak Level

- RMS Level

- Noise Floor.

The steps provided will show how to ensure that the criteria passed the strict requirements.

The Noise Floor may show as a warning, but not a fail. A warning is still a pass.   With spoken word content, the silence between sentences could generate a warning. That is nothing to worry about. It's when you see a "fail" when you should focus on fixing the problem.

Audacity Settings & Criteria

It's easy to find Audacity settings and criteria by searching videos online.

Search for:

"Recording audiobook with audacity"

To help save time, certain setting adjustments will be shown here.

The following pages are presented in 'note' to be brief and to the point. They are also presented in relevant order.

The steps provided in order help to maximize quality required for ACX's highest standards of all aggregators for audiobook content are summarized here, but detail and tutorials can be found in online videos.

The steps are:

- Noise Reduction

- Loudness Normalization

- Compressor

- Limiter

- Silence (Start End)

These are the elements in terms of "effects" to focus on to maximize the quality of the Audio books. These effects can be found on video tutorials online, but let's take a look at specific settings and parameters relevant to audiobook production.

[1] Effect > Noise Reduction

These are the initial steps

- Step 1: Get noise profile first by highlighting background Noise

- Step 2: Remove noise

Here are the settings.

--- Noise reduction (dB): 6** (based on room noise - Need to be -60db)

--- Sensitivity: 6.00

--- Frequency Smoothing (bands): 6

--- Noise Reduce (not Residue)

- Step 3: Remove room noise recording at the end.

Determine the noise reduction parameter by subtracting the level that you see from the mic from 60. If you see -40, then the noise reduction parameter is -20.   If you see -35, then the noise reduction parameter is 25.   It's OK to make the noise floor -65 dB or -70 dB to ensure you aren't cutting it too close to the -60 dB line.

[2] Effect > Loudness Normalization

Here are the settings:

-- Normalize [**RMS**] to -20 LUFS

-- (check box): Normalize stereo channels independently

-- (check box): Treat mono as dual-mono (recommended)

[3] Effect > Compressor >

Here are the settings.

- Threshold -12 db

- Noise Floor -40 db

- Ratio 5.1:1 (***important***)

- Attack Time 0.20 secs

- Release Time 1.0 secs

- NOTE: Do not check boxes

--- uncheck: Make-up gain for 0db

--- uncheck: Compress based on

Peaks

[4] Effect > Limiter

Here are the settings:

- Type: Soft Limit

- Input Gain (dB): mono/Left = 0.00

- input Gain (dB): Right Channel = 0.00

- Limit to (dB): -3.00 (***important***)

- Hold (ms): 1.00 (one point zero)

- Apply Make-Up Gain: No

[5] Header and Footer

Header Space

All tracks must start between 0.5 to 1 second of silence at the beginning of the track. Recommend using 0.8 seconds of silence on the front of tracks to ensure 100 percent compliance

[6] Starting Header Space

All tracks must start between 0.5 to 1 second of silence at the beginning of the track. Recommend using 0.8 seconds of silence on the front of tracks to ensure 100 percent compliance

[7] Ending Footer Space

All tracks must end with between 1 to 5 seconds of silence at the ending. We recommend using 3 seconds of silence on the end of tracks to ensure 100 percent compliance.

Header = 0.8 and Footer = 3.0

A silent part of a track can be added.

You can create silence

Generate > Silence

If RMS is too low, amplify by 1.0

Adjust in Audacity to amplify

Here is the selection to amplify

within Audacity.

Effects>Amplify

<u>Nyquist ACX Check Plugin</u>

Remember to download and install the ACX Check Plugin

https://wiki.audacityteam.org/wiki/Nyquist_Analyze_Plug-ins

Analyze > ACX Check (You want PASS)

If you see a warning, that does not mean a failure.   You might see a "warning" for room noise too low or too quiet as being not natural. That is OK. It is not a failure.

<u>Conclusion</u>

What we see here are some basic tools for professional public speakers who are also authors of their own books with a recorded audiobook. Along with an online presence that is professional on at least LinkedIn and Twitter with a do-it-yourself website containing a domain name will package nicely a public speaker. As with everything it takes practice. Examples given included podcasting and video recording to ensure a final presentation to go smoothly. Even Hollywood actors must do a couple of takes to get it right. Good preparation is the key.

The process of recording an audiobook includes methods to help proactively conquer the professional spoken language.

That being said, it is worthy to put attention into them. They also serve as an accolade and distinction. Many speakers have books, but fewer have audiobooks. And audiobooks are a segment of publishing that is growing.

David K. Ewen, M.Ed.

Ambassador Professor

Enterprise College

www.EnterpriseCollege.org

Public Speaking Greatness

Power Communication to Your Advantage

By

David K. Ewen, M.Ed.

ISBN: 9798406299333

Imprint: Enterprise College

www.EnterpriseCollege.org

Cover theme background
El Cap, Yosemite National Park, United States
Produced by: Adam Cool
Published on March 17, 2015

Contents

<u>About the Book</u>

Public Speaking Greatness brings the tips, tricks, and techniques to improve your public speaking style to greater performance to bring greater impact to your audiences. The methods brought on by an international award-winning educator will change your stance in the public arena.

David K. Ewen, M.Ed.

Ambassador Professor

Enterprise College

www.EnterpriseCollege.org

<u>About the author</u>

The acclaimed sought-after international award-winning David K. Ewen, M.Ed., an acclaimed educator since 1988, an entrepreneur since 1994, an Ambassador Professor since 2015 and ordained minister since 2021, has been a professional speaker in front of LIVE audiences, classrooms, broadcast radio, streaming podcast, and at church altars.

David is the author of several books and audiobooks on a variety of professional issues. David's specialty is in global communications and entrepreneurial studies. In addition to speaking in front of live audiences, he creates and presents classroom workshop seminars and online masterclass webinars.   In the EdTech industry (education technology), David is a content creator developing curriculum which he presents in online coaching sessions and masterclass webinars.   He earned a master's degree in education with a concentration in management and attended post graduate studies in business administration before he launched his publishing company in

July 1994.

Cover theme background
El Cap, Yosemite National Park, United States
Produced by: Adam Cool
Published on March 17, 2015

David K. Ewen, M.Ed.

Ambassador Professor

Enterprise College

www.EnterpriseCollege.org